SPRING EDITION

My Daily
Word

read · reflect · renew

DEVOTIONAL

My Daily Word
Read. Reflect. Renew

Copyright© 2017 by Inprov, Ltd.
ISBN: 978-0-9963685-2-0

For further information, write Inprov, at:
2150 E. Continental Blvd, Southlake, TX 76092

My Daily Word is a unique daily devotional featuring a daily reading plan, a quick inspirational thought and a special designated space for you to journal your thoughts and prayers for each day.

Divided into four editions – spring, summer, fall and winter – this devotional will encourage you in your faith and help you grow in your relationship with the Lord as you read through the Bible.

Whether you choose to start or end your day in God's Word, you will truly look forward to reading it every day.

READ IT: Psalm 143:1-12

Let the morning bring me word of your unfailing love, for I have put my trust in you. Show me the way I should go, for to you I entrust my life (Psalm 143:8).

THINK ABOUT IT: Remember this morning and every morning to put your trust in the Lord and His unfailing love. Trust that He will make your path clear as you entrust your life to Him. His love will never fail you – believe that today!

MARCH
2

READ IT: John 10:22-42

"I give them eternal life, and they shall never perish; no one will snatch them out of my hand. My Father, who has given them to me, is greater than all; no one can snatch them out of my Father's hand" (John 10:28-29).

THINK ABOUT IT: God is bigger and stronger than any adversity that may come against you today or any day. Rest in the comfort of knowing that you are held in the palm of the Father's hand and that no powers of darkness are strong enough to pull you away from that. Nothing will ever compare to being in the presence of our Father and feeling the confidence of having Him on your side.

READ IT: Exodus 3:1-22

God said to Moses, "I AM WHO I AM. This is what you are to say to the Israelites: 'I AM has sent me to you'" (Exodus 3:14).

THINK ABOUT IT: It's easy to be like Moses when God calls you to do something. You may give God excuses about not feeling qualified or adequate, or you may be afraid of failure or filled with self-doubt. But your feelings won't change who God is: "I AM." Your wisdom, your strength, your abilities — no matter where they fall — won't matter in the end, because it is God who will do the work. It is His strength that works through your weakness, and you only need to submit to Him and the power He has to work in any situation.

MARCH
4

READ IT: Psalm 66:1-16

Come and hear, all you who fear God; let me tell you what he has done for me (Psalm 66:16).

THINK ABOUT IT: God shows up in all sorts of ways – often in ways we are not even aware of. This psalmist continually rejoices in the presence and power of God. No matter what you face today, rejoice in the Lord. God hears your prayers, and His love is not withheld from you. Embrace the comfort and joy that comes through praising our Lord.

READ IT: Romans 8:18-27

In the same way, the Spirit helps us in our weakness. We do not know what we ought to pray for, but the Spirit himself intercedes for us through wordless groans (Romans 8:26).

THINK ABOUT IT: You may not know the words to pray today, but rest in the knowledge that we are loved by a Father who so intimately knows our hearts. He knit us together, and He hears what is on your heart today. Do you feel a longing for something that you are unable to articulate? When we are weak, God is strong. Lean into His strength and trust that the Spirit will move through you to communicate your wordless prayers today.

MARCH
6

READ IT: 2 Corinthians 4:1-12

We are hard pressed on every side, but not crushed; perplexed, but not in despair; persecuted, but not abandoned; struck down, but not destroyed (2 Corinthians 4:8-9).

THINK ABOUT IT: Defeat is not an option. No matter what adversities you face, place your hope in the Lord today and see that because of His love and strength, you are empowered to push through every difficult situation. You are not crushed or in despair – God is for you. You are not abandoned – God is with you. You are not destroyed – God is your Protector. Trust that He is bigger than whatever you are facing.

READ IT: Nahum 1:2-15
The LORD is good, a refuge in times of trouble (Nahum 1:7).

THINK ABOUT IT: No matter what you are facing today, know that God is a refuge for you. All He asks of us is to trust in Him, to turn to Him in not only our times of need, but also in our times of rejoicing. We are blessed with a Father who delights in being our Father. Put your trust in God, and know that He will be a refuge for you today.

READ IT: John 15:8-17

"This is to my Father's glory, that you bear much fruit, showing yourselves to be my disciples. As the Father has loved me, so have I loved you. Now remain in my love" (John 15:8-9).

THINK ABOUT IT: Jesus commands us to love one another – and by extending love toward others, we will bear fruit in our lives. The more you remain in the love of Jesus, the easier it is to spread that same love to those around you. Remind yourself to return to God's love today – and as He loves you, so should you love others.

READ IT: Psalm 103:1-14

As a father has compassion on his children, so the LORD has compassion on those who fear him; for he knows how we are formed, he remembers that we are dust (Psalm 103:13-14).

THINK ABOUT IT: In this Psalm of David, we are reminded that God is a perfect Father for imperfect children. We have a loving God full of compassion and forgiveness. He intimately knows every piece of us, yet He still loves us. Turn toward the love of our Father today and feel His compassion for you.

MARCH
10

READ IT: Colossians 2:6-15

. . . having canceled the charge of our legal indebtedness, which stood against us and condemned us; he has taken it away, nailing it to the cross. And having disarmed the powers and authorities, he made a public spectacle of them, triumphing over them by the cross (Colossians 2:14-15).

THINK ABOUT IT: The enemy only has the power to shame us if we give it to him, and the antidote to shame is the love of Christ. Ask God to give you eyes to see where there are still dark areas in your soul. Turn to your rescuer. Turn away from shame, and see your deliverer today.

"He who knew no shame took our shame upon Him so you and I could be free. It's called grace – unmerited favor."

—Sheila Walsh

READ IT: **2 TImothy 2:1-13**
. . . if we are faithless, he remains faithful, for he cannot disown himself (2 Timothy 2:13).

THINK ABOUT IT: Our God is eternally faithful even when we fall short. It's all about Him and never about us. Remember that we are called to love God and one another, and remember to let the light and love of Christ shine through you today.

MARCH
12

READ IT: James 4:1-6

But he gives us more grace. That is why Scripture says: "God opposes the proud but shows favor to the humble" (James 4:6).

THINK ABOUT IT: Humble yourself before the Lord today and receive the grace that we are freely given. This section in James tells us that a spirit of humility will bring us closer to the Lord and that we will be lifted up. If you are facing any uncertainty in your life today, submit yourself to God and trust in His will. Remain in a position of humility and know that He is greater than whatever you may be facing.

MARCH
13

READ IT: Luke 21:5-37

"Everyone will hate you because of me. But not a hair of your head will perish. Stand firm, and you will win life" (Luke 21:17-19).

THINK ABOUT IT: We are told in Scripture that we will face trials because of our identity in Christ. You will encounter people who don't understand, people who disagree and people who may even mock. However, Jesus calls us to stand firm in our faith. Turn to God when you feel that the world is against you, and remember that your hope rests in Jesus.

READ IT: 1 John 1:7-10

If we confess our sins, he is faithful and just and will forgive us our sins and purify us from all unrighteousness (1 John 1:9).

THINK ABOUT IT: You may find yourself carrying the weight of past sins today. The good news is that we are already forgiven because of Jesus' sacrifice. We were forgiven the moment He died on the cross. When this verse says to "confess our sins," it doesn't mean to ask for forgiveness — we've already received forgiveness. We are told simply to call our sin what it is and confess it to God. To acknowledge our sins will bring us closer to Him.

READ IT: **Romans 5:1-11**

Not only so, but we also glory in our sufferings, because we know that suffering produces perseverance; perseverance, character; and character, hope (Romans 5:3-4).

THINK ABOUT IT: Remaining positive and even joyful through sufferings can be a difficult task; however, Paul writes in Romans that we must glory and rejoice in our sufferings because they produce perseverance, character and hope. When suffering produces hope, it builds confidence in a God who loves us. God is big enough to cover anything you are facing today. Let any negative feelings be transformed into perseverance, character and hope. Know that God loves you, train your mind to turn to Him through your suffering, and rejoice that it is building up a greater purpose within you.

MARCH
16

READ IT: 2 Corinthians 5:18-21

God made him who had no sin to be sin for us, so that in him we might become the righteousness of God (2 Corinthians 5:21).

THINK ABOUT IT: This verse shows us everything we need to know about Jesus' sacrifice for us. Jesus, God's one and only Son, became sin on our behalf so that we could become whole. Our flesh will fail over and over, but we are redeemed through the gift of Christ. Remember today that you have the opportunity to become the righteousness of God. Rejoice in the knowledge that you can be made whole through this gift!

READ IT: **Genesis 3:1-13**

Then the eyes of both of them were opened, and they realized they were naked; so they sewed fig leaves together and made coverings for themselves. Then the man and his wife heard the sound of the LORD God as he was walking in the garden in the cool of the day, and they hid from the LORD God among the trees of the garden (Genesis 3:7-8).

THINK ABOUT IT: When we sin, we feel naked in our shame. Like Adam and Eve, instead of running to God, we try to hide from Him. Know today that His love and goodness are bigger than your sin and shame. How can you use negative feelings to motivate yourself to turn toward God and trust that His love covers all shortcomings?

MARCH
18

READ IT: Jeremiah 17:5-18
"They will be like a tree planted by the water that sends out its roots by the stream. It does not fear when heat comes; its leaves are always green. It has no worries in a year of drought and never fails to bear fruit" (Jeremiah 17:8).

THINK ABOUT IT: When we put our trust and confidence in the Lord, we flourish like the tree planted by the water. We know that Jesus is living water, and when our roots drink from Him, we bear fruit. From where are your roots absorbing nutrients? Where are you placing your trust and confidence today? Turn to God and know that He is where we receive LIFE!

READ IT: **Psalm 55:16-23**
Cast your cares on the LORD and he will sustain you; he will never let the righteous be shaken (Psalm 55:22).

THINK ABOUT IT: Have you ever felt shaken by your current circumstances? We are told that He will never let us be shaken. As long as we keep our hope in Him and trust that He cares for and sustains us, we will not be shaken by whatever we may face. But will you allow yourself to be shaken by things that are of this world? Cast your cares, worries and stress on God, and trust that all will be taken care of through His strength.

READ IT: 1 Peter 5:1-10

Cast all your anxiety on him because he cares for you (1 Peter 5:7).

THINK ABOUT IT: This simple direction from Peter can seem so difficult at times. We live in a world that breeds stress and anxiety, and to simply cast it all aside sounds so easy. But that can be so difficult to do. You are loved by a Father who calls you His own. Even when you feel small, unnoticed or unloved, Jesus is always there, ready to take your daily burdens. A life of peace and joy is at your fingertips; all you have to do is trust that the Lord cares for you and is ready to take on all of your anxieties.

"Bring what feels so out of control to God, knowing He is good and He loves you, and trust Him with the timing. Bring the thing that you long to fix to God, give it to Him and trust Him with the outcome."

—Sheila Walsh

MARCH
21

READ IT: Genesis 3:20-24

And the LORD God said, "The man has now become like one of us, knowing good and evil. He must not be allowed to reach out his hand and take also from the tree of life and eat, and live forever." So the LORD God banished him from the Garden of Eden to work the ground from which he had been taken (Genesis 3:22-23).

THINK ABOUT IT: God loves us so much that He kept us from an eternity of brokenness. Had He allowed Adam and Eve to remain in the garden, they would have lived forever broken. The good news is that we are made whole through Jesus, and now we get to live that eternity with God — reunited as He always intended.

READ IT: Ephesians 6:10-20

Finally, be strong in the Lord and in his mighty power. Put on the full armor of God, so that you can take your stand against the devil's schemes (Ephesians 6:10-11).

THINK ABOUT IT: Intentionally put on the armor of God today, piece by piece, and see what God works in your life. With God on your side, anything is possible, and the devil has no power over you. Our Lord is stronger than any powers of darkness that may try to work against you today. The Lord's strength will work through you today!

READ IT: Luke 9:57-62

Jesus replied, "No one who puts a hand to the plow and looks back is fit for service in the kingdom of God" (Luke 9:62).

THINK ABOUT IT: The only way to see a great harvest in your life is to keep your eyes on God. The moment you take your attention away from Him and allow distractions into your line of vision, your plow is no longer moving in a straight line. Refocus your attention on the Lord today and see how He uses you to serve the Kingdom!

MARCH
24

READ IT: Matthew 6:5-14

"Do not be like them, for your Father knows what you need before you ask him" (Matthew 6:8).

THINK ABOUT IT: This passage includes instructions from Jesus on how to pray. He urges us to not pray to be seen or heard by others and to not pray by babbling like pagans. Jesus says that the Father knows what you need before you ever ask Him. Your prayer life is your personal line of communication with God. He knows your heart in this moment, so let your prayer flow freely from that. Rather than praying to be heard or seen by others, pray so that you feel the intimacy of a conversation with your Father.

READ IT: Revelation 22:12-21

He who testifies to these things says, "Yes, I am coming soon."
Amen. Come, Lord Jesus (Revelation 22:20).

THINK ABOUT IT: Life is full of uncertainty, and it is so easy to get caught up in the anxieties of the unknown. We are left with a beautiful promise at the close of Revelation. Jesus says, "Yes, I am coming soon." We serve a God who was and is and is to come, and this is the only promise of the future we need. Jesus will return, and you can place your hope in His return today. Rest in His promises.

MARCH
26

READ IT: John 12:20-36

"Anyone who loves their life will lose it, while anyone who hates their life in this world will keep it for eternal life" (John 12:25).

THINK ABOUT IT: As Christians, we are called to lay down our lives for Christ – not to live for ourselves, but rather to live a life of service. The path of a Christ follower is not always an easy one. We are not called to live in the moment, distracted by the temptations of this world, but rather we are called to live for the life that is to come – an eternity with our Heavenly Father.

READ IT: 1 Corinthians 1:1-9

I always thank my God for you because of his grace given you in Christ Jesus. For in him you have been enriched in every way – with all kinds of speech and with all knowledge . . . (1 Corinthians 1:4-5)

THINK ABOUT IT: Paul writes of his thankfulness to God in 1 Corinthians, addressing issues within the church but never forgetting to be grateful to God. He acknowledges that while there are problems that need to be corrected, through God's grace, there is still so much good coming out of the Corinthians. They have been enriched in every way – and so have you! We will always fall short, but be grateful today that by the grace of God, our lives are enriched!

MARCH
28

READ IT: Psalm 91:1-16

He will cover you with his feathers, and under his wings you will find refuge; his faithfulness will be your shield and rampart (Psalm 91:4).

THINK ABOUT IT: We are not told that we will never face adversity in life, but we are told that God will be a place of refuge for us in the midst of it all. It's His faithfulness, His devotion to His children, that will equip you to persevere through any challenge you may be facing. Feel His love around you today and trust that His strength is a shield against anything that may come against you.

MARCH
29

READ IT: John 6:25-59

Then Jesus declared, "I am the bread of life. Whoever comes to me will never go hungry, and whoever believes in me will never be thirsty" (John 6:35).

THINK ABOUT IT: The Lord is your Shepherd; you shall not want. God promises to be your sustenance. He will provide for your every need – your physical hunger and thirst, but also your spiritual hunger and thirst. You may be looking for something more in your life today, but fix your eyes on Jesus and see that He is all you need.

READ IT: Genesis 8:18-22

"As long as the earth endures, seedtime and harvest, cold and heat, summer and winter, day and night will never cease" (Genesis 8:22).

THINK ABOUT IT: Even in Genesis after the flood, God reveals His faithfulness and trustworthiness. After Noah offers the Lord a sacrifice that pleases Him, He promises, "Never again will I curse the ground." God desires that we know and understand how to live fruitful lives. We can count on God to keep His promises to us just like we can count on the arrivals and departures of each season.

"No matter how great your longing is for God, it will never, ever, ever compare to God's longing for you."

—Sheila Walsh

MARCH
31

READ IT: 2 Corinthians 10:1-17

We demolish arguments and every pretension that sets itself up against the knowledge of God, and we take captive every thought to make it obedient to Christ (2 Corinthians 10:5).

THINK ABOUT IT: Taking your thoughts captive may sound like a challenge. You are probably familiar with thoughts of inadequacy or failure or self-doubt. Some days you may feel plagued by these kinds of thoughts, but rather than letting those thoughts take you captive, you are called to take the thoughts captive. Every time a thought like this enters your mind, take a moment to ask where the thought is coming from. If you know it is not from God, then demolish it. Train your thoughts to be obedient to God, and learn to discern the truth that comes from the Father from the lies that come from the enemy.

APRIL
1

READ IT: Romans 12:1-8

Do not conform to the pattern of this world, but be transformed by the renewing of your mind. Then you will be able to test and approve what God's will is – his good, pleasing and perfect will (Romans 12:2).

THINK ABOUT IT: Once again we are called to keep our eyes on God and avoid the distractions of the world we live in. Allow the grace and power of the Lord to renew your mind so that you may thrive in the joy that comes only from a personal relationship with your Heavenly Father. God's will for your life is perfect! Allow Him to renew your mind today.

READ IT: Daniel 6:1-28

"My God sent his angel, and he shut the mouths of the lions. They have not hurt me, because I was found innocent in his sight. Nor have I ever done any wrong before you, Your Majesty" (Daniel 6:22).

THINK ABOUT IT: Daniel was thrown into a pit of lions and left overnight because of his devotion to God. You may think that you deserve to be rewarded for doing the right thing; but we live in a broken world, and you may have to face opposition. It is up to you to trust God even when you're thrown into a situation that is as hostile as a pit of lions. Remain committed to doing what is right, and be obedient to the Lord when the world turns against you.

APRIL
3

READ IT: Hebrews 13:6-18

So we say with confidence, "The Lord is my helper; I will not be afraid. What can mere mortals do to me?" (Hebrews 13:6)

THINK ABOUT IT: We are promised that the Lord will never leave us nor forsake us. We are loved by a God who promises unwavering, unfailing love and support for us, so know today that there is nothing to fear. Nothing in this world will ever come close to the power and glory of our Father, so live your life assured of the confidence that comes through putting your faith and hope in Him.

READ IT: James 5:13-20

Therefore confess your sins to each other and pray for each other so that you may be healed. The prayer of a righteous person is powerful and effective (James 5:16).

THINK ABOUT IT: What kind of people have you surrounded yourself with? Community is important to the Christian life, as made abundantly clear in the fellowship Jesus shared with His disciples and in the early churches that formed as a result. Accountability is important within these communities. There is strength within the body of Christ, so surround yourself with supportive Christians, and hold one another accountable.

APRIL
5

READ IT: Ephesians 4:17-32

Be kind and compassionate to one another, forgiving each other, just as in Christ God forgave you (Ephesians 4:32).

THINK ABOUT IT: In Ephesians chapter 4, Paul warns about the toxicity that comes through anger. Get rid of any anger, bitterness or rage that you are feeling right now. Give those negative feelings to God and remember the forgiveness you received when Jesus died on the cross. Freely give that forgiveness to others today. Stop holding on to the bad feelings that are weighing you down, and extend kindness and compassion to yourself and others.

READ IT: John 8:1-11

"Then neither do I condemn you," Jesus declared. "Go now and leave your life of sin" (John 8:11).

THINK ABOUT IT: Nothing will ever separate you from the love of God. You are promised His companionship for all the days of your life. While we are called to leave a life of sin, we live in a sinful and broken world. Know that you are not condemned today for any of the sin in your life – you are LOVED. Choose to walk in the Father's grace today, not in condemnation.

APRIL
7

READ IT: James 3:1-12
Likewise, the tongue is a small part of the body, but it makes great boasts. Consider what a great forest is set on fire by a small spark (James 3:5).

THINK ABOUT IT: Be mindful of your words today. God has empowered you with a mind capable of processing every word before it leaves the tip of your tongue. When we are not careful, we can spark a blaze of hurt, anger or sadness for others with a single word. The power of the tongue is very strong, and we are warned to be careful with that power. Challenge yourself to speak words of kindness and compassion to those around you today.

READ IT: Colossians 1:9-18

For he has rescued us from the dominion of darkness and brought us into the kingdom of the Son he loves . . . (Colossians 1:13)

THINK ABOUT IT: We are rescued, and we are free – all because of Jesus! Does your life reflect that belief? Are you living in the knowledge that you are not confined under any powers of darkness? Start today. Believe that Christ has rescued you. Know that any darkness that you may encounter has no power over the mighty power of God.

READ IT: Nehemiah 8:1-11

Nehemiah said, "Go and enjoy choice food and sweet drinks, and send some to those who have nothing prepared. This day is holy to our Lord. Do not grieve, for the joy of the LORD is your strength" (Nehemiah 8:10).

THINK ABOUT IT: The joy of the Lord is your strength! Every day is created by God, so don't live your life as if there is nothing to rejoice in. Surely you will face trying times and challenges, but find strength in the knowledge that our joy comes from the Lord — an ever-present help and an unfailing love! Feel the strength that comes from that joy today, and let it carry you through any difficulties you may be facing.

"Every single day, if we could pray this prayer: God, give me eyes to see today what I would miss, and give me ears to hear beyond what somebody is saying to what is going on in their heart."

—Sheila Walsh

READ IT: 1 Timothy 6:3-10
For we brought nothing into the world, and we can take nothing out of it (1 Timothy 6:7).

THINK ABOUT IT: The fullness of life comes through knowing God – it is only through Jesus that we are made whole and complete. A lot of times people think that if only they had more money or more possessions they would be happier or more content, but time and time again this fails. You know that the Lord will meet your every need. Simply trust in Him and His will for your life, and you will feel the fullness and contentment that comes from being in His presence.

READ IT: 1 Corinthians 10:23-33
No one should seek their own good, but the good of others
(1 Corinthians 10:24).

THINK ABOUT IT: What can you do today to intentionally seek the good of others? When was the last time you helped someone to grow in their relationship with Jesus? We have freedom through Christ, yet we are called to lift up those around us, and sometimes that requires sacrifice. However, you will often find that when you sacrifice for the good of those around you, you will reap the fruit of that relationship and grow in your own relationship with Christ.

APRIL
12

READ IT: Hebrews 12:1-11

Consider him who endured such opposition from sinners, so that you will not grow weary and lose heart (Hebrews 12:3).

THINK ABOUT IT: Your life is like a race, a path carved out by God on which we must run. You will encounter obstacles, stretches of time where you feel exhausted, and other hindrances. However, we are called to persevere through those difficulties and run the race. Set your eyes on Jesus and recall all that He endured for you today – let that motivate you to push through the tough spots and avoid losing heart. He is cheering you on and running right alongside you!

APRIL
13

READ IT: John 15:1-5

"I am the vine; you are the branches. If you remain in me and I in you, you will bear much fruit; apart from me you can do nothing" (John 15:5).

THINK ABOUT IT: It is through Christ that we are able to accomplish anything in life. You can try to depend on yourself, but our flesh fails. It is the supernatural power and love of our Father that enables us to reap what we sow. Live your life through Him as an extended branch from the vine. Acknowledge where your nutrients and sustenance come from, and you will thrive.

READ IT: **Matthew 10:27-33**
"And even the very hairs of your head are all numbered"
(Matthew 10:30).

THINK ABOUT IT: It is hard to imagine being so loved by a
Father that He knows the number of hairs on your head. Yet we are
told that we were knit together, piece by piece, by a God who truly
loves and cares for us. His love never fails. Rest in that belief today.
The love of God cannot be compared to anything in this world.

READ IT: Colossians 3:12-17

Bear with each other and forgive one another if any of you has a grievance against someone. Forgive as the Lord forgave you (Colossians 3:13).

THINK ABOUT IT: Forgiveness can be so difficult. God knows that forgiveness can be scary or painful or even seem impossible at times. However, Jesus died on the cross so that forgiveness would be extended to the ends of the earth. We were given the greatest sacrifice so that we could experience the love and mercy of our Father. Remember the forgiveness you have been given, and strive to extend the same to those around you today.

APRIL
16

READ IT: John 14:27-31

"Peace I leave with you; my peace I give you. I do not give to you as the world gives. Do not let your hearts be troubled and do not be afraid" (John 14:27).

THINK ABOUT IT: The heavenly gifts we receive from God surpass any gifts this world can offer. Feel the peace of God's grace over you and see how it supernaturally affects your life today.

APRIL
17

READ IT: Matthew 6:24-27
"Can any one of you by worrying add a single hour to your life?"
(Matthew 6:27)

THINK ABOUT IT: Worrying won't help you solve any problems. It isn't helpful, necessary or even natural; in fact, it can oftentimes be harmful, causing stress and anxiety. What are you worrying about today? Maybe it is your health, your bills or the choices of someone else. No matter what you feel worried about, challenge yourself to let go of that worry, and trust that all of your needs will be met through Christ.

READ IT: **Psalm 23:1-6**

He makes me lie down in green pastures, he leads me beside quiet waters, he refreshes my soul (Psalm 23:2-3).

THINK ABOUT IT: The Lord is your Shepherd! Feel the refreshing of your soul as you fix your eyes on Jesus today. Imagine walking with Him by still, quiet waters surrounded by green pastures. You are fulfilled in every way because of our God who provides for you. Remember this peaceful picture today. Remind yourself that you are not alone – the Lord is leading you today and every day that follows.

APRIL
19

READ IT: 1 John 1:1-6

If we claim to have fellowship with him and yet walk in the darkness, we lie and do not live out the truth (1 John 1:6).

THINK ABOUT IT: Are you walking in darkness? What are you carrying with you today that God is inviting you to relinquish to Him and His power? If you have Jesus in your life and in your heart, you don't have to walk anywhere but with Him in His light. Fellowship with the Lord today and walk in the light. How can you be a light in the darkness that envelops those around you?

"The mystery of the gift of grace: it shows up just when you need it. Not a moment too soon, but not a moment too late."

—Sheila Walsh

READ IT: Matthew 5:1-16

"In the same way, let your light shine before others, that they may see your good deeds and glorify your Father in heaven" (Matthew 5:16).

THINK ABOUT IT: How different do you look from your coworkers, your family, your friends or anyone you encounter on a daily basis? Do you stand apart because of your light? The people of this broken world long for the light they do not yet know. Don't keep the glory of God to yourself – share it with everyone you meet. Let your light shine!

READ IT: Romans 1:18-32

For although they knew God, they neither glorified him as God nor gave thanks to him, but their thinking became futile and their foolish hearts were darkened (Romans 1:21).

THINK ABOUT IT: This is such a sad picture of people who knew God yet chose to live for themselves. Don't choose the temptations of the world over all that God has to offer for your life. Glorify the Lord in your words and actions today. Thank Him for the blessings that surround you. Remain in His light so that you may be a light for others.

READ IT: **2 Timothy 3:1-17**
All Scripture is God-breathed and is useful for teaching, rebuking, correcting and training in righteousness . . . (2 Timothy 3:16)

THINK ABOUT IT: Be consistent with your time spent in God's Word. Scripture is a gift from God – a great tool with which to learn. Without learning, there is no growth. In order to continue to grow as a Christ follower, use the tools you are equipped with, especially Scripture! You can read the same verse over and over and get new things each time you read it. Remain steadfast in your learning and see how your world changes.

READ IT: John 14:1-4

"You know the way to the place where I am going" (John 14:4).

THINK ABOUT IT: God has revealed to us how to have eternal life with Him, and Jesus confirms that we know the way there. Are you living like you know the way? It is given to us in Scripture. Reflect on the wisdom that Jesus freely imparts to His disciples. He has shown us the way to follow Him. We simply have to live a life that acknowledges this.

READ IT: **Hebrews 10:19-24**

And let us consider how we may spur one another on toward love and good deeds . . . (Hebrews 10:24)

THINK ABOUT IT: When was the last time you encouraged someone around you? We are called to live in love and commit good deeds, but we are also called to encourage those around us to do the same. Invest in a community; find people who will also support you. Surround yourself with love and encouragement, and it will flow from you freely.

READ IT: 1 John 2:15-23

The world and its desires pass away, but whoever does the will of God lives forever (1 John 2:17).

THINK ABOUT IT: Where are you placing your trust and confidence today? What desires have you acted on recently? Have your actions brought you closer to God? The things of this world will not last; we are told that the world will fade away. Place your trust in the Lord and set your eyes on the eternity that you have to look forward to. When your actions move through this mindset, you will feel yourself grow in your relationship with God.

READ IT: Psalm 32:1-11

You are my hiding place; you will protect me from trouble and surround me with songs of deliverance (Psalm 32:7).

THINK ABOUT IT: Do you ever feel like you need a break from the pressures and demands of your daily life? Turn to God in those moments, and know that He is your hiding place. Rest in the stillness, peace and comfort that He offers, and trust in His protection over your life. Take a break with the Lord today.

APRIL
27

READ IT: 1 John 4:9-16

And so we know and rely on the love God has for us. God is love.
Whoever lives in love lives in God, and God in them (1 John 4:16).

THINK ABOUT IT: This world will fail you, but God will
not. His love is steady and unwavering, and when it feels like
everything is crashing down around you, turn to Him and live in
the love He freely extends to you. Rely on that love to pull you
through. Trust that God lives in you, enabling you to extend that
love to those around you.

READ IT: Joshua 3:1-17

Joshua told the people, "Consecrate yourselves, for tomorrow the LORD will do amazing things among you" (Joshua 3:5).

THINK ABOUT IT: So often we find ourselves wanting to do great and amazing things for God. However, this verse tells us that it is the Lord who will do amazing things for us. We are simply asked to consecrate ourselves, give of ourselves freely to Him, and prepare for the work He is sure to do in us and through us. Stop trying to please God, and know that He already loves you. There is nothing you can do to make Him love you any more or any less than He already does. Watch Him work in your life.

READ IT: 1 Timothy 1:12-14

Even though I was once a blasphemer and a persecutor and a violent man, I was shown mercy because I acted in ignorance and unbelief (1 Timothy 1:13).

THINK ABOUT IT: Your past does not dictate your future. Blasphemers and persecutors and violent people can be transformed through the power of Christ. Whether that is you or someone in your life, believe that God has an endless supply of mercy. We were forgiven when Jesus gave His life. Walk boldly today in the knowledge that you are transformed by God's grace over your life.

"Everything you crave – the good and the bad – ultimately leads you to the heart of God, to your Father who loves you right now, just where you are."

—Sheila Walsh

READ IT: Isaiah 54:1-17

" . . . no weapon forged against you will prevail, and you will refute every tongue that accuses you. This is the heritage of the servants of the LORD, and this is their vindication from me," declares the LORD *(Isaiah 54:17).*

THINK ABOUT IT: The Lord has declared that no weapon forged against you will prevail. As a believer, you are equipped with the armor of God, and no matter what you face or what may come against you, you can have victory because of Jesus! Through Him you are made strong and empowered to fight against any attacks.

MAY
1

READ IT: Romans 8:1-11

Therefore, there is now no condemnation for those who are in Christ Jesus, because through Christ Jesus the law of the Spirit who gives life has set you free from the law of sin and death (Romans 8:1-2).

THINK ABOUT IT: Because of Jesus, you are free to live a life covered by His grace. You are not condemned for any past or future actions; you are free through Christ. Today know that no matter how you may feel about yourself, God does not condemn you. Allow your mind to be Kingdom-focused. This doesn't mean we should sin freely and without worry; it means that when we inevitably fail, the Lord's love will not stop flowing over us.

READ IT: **Psalm 139:1-24**

For you created my inmost being; you knit me together in my mother's womb (Psalm 139:13).

THINK ABOUT IT: You never have to feel unloved or inadequate when you have a relationship with God. He knows every piece of you – even the pieces you hide away and keep secret from people – and yet He still loves you immensely. He knit you together in your mother's womb and created you with a purpose. You are known and loved by our Heavenly Father who put you together piece by piece.

MAY
3

READ IT: Romans 10:14-21

Consequently, faith comes from hearing the message, and the message is heard through the word about Christ (Romans 10:17).

THINK ABOUT IT: Spend time this week reading Scripture out loud to yourself, and see how your faith is increased. Scripture is a tool at your fingertips that can teach you and help you grow in your relationship with Christ. Let yourself hear the promises of God from your own mouth, and come to know them with your heart and mind!

READ IT: **Genesis 50:1-21**
"You intended to harm me, but God intended it for good to accomplish what is now being done, the saving of many lives" (Genesis 50:20).

THINK ABOUT IT: How do you act when you go through a trial? Joseph was confident in God's will for his life, resting in the knowledge that God works all things for His good. It can be hard to see the good in the midst of the bad, but God has promised to never leave you. Believe that! He is right there; He is the only good you need to see. What testimony can you share of a time that God worked something good through a difficult time in your life?

READ IT: 1 John 4:17-21

There is no fear in love. But perfect love drives out fear, because fear has to do with punishment. The one who fears is not made perfect in love (1 John 4:18).

THINK ABOUT IT: We are told in Scripture that God is love – His whole being is love, and that love is poured out onto all of us. The more you commune with God and embrace the love He freely gives, the less fear you will have in your life. God's perfect love drives out any fears or anxieties that may be holding you back. What do you fear most? Know that God is bigger than that fear – and His love is great enough to cover all fear today.

READ IT: Hebrews 11:23-29

He regarded disgrace for the sake of Christ as of greater value than the treasures of Egypt, because he was looking ahead to his reward (Hebrews 11:26).

THINK ABOUT IT: Even when Moses did not fully understand what all God had in store for his future, he kept his eyes fixed ahead and avoided the distraction and temptations of earthly affluence. Moses' actions should be an example today and a reminder to look ahead to what God has in store for you. Even though you don't fully know or understand, you can be sure that His will for your life is greater than anything this world can offer you.

MAY
7

READ IT: Philippians 2:1-11

In your relationships with one another, have the same mindset as Christ Jesus . . . (Philippians 2:5)

THINK ABOUT IT: This is such a difficult call to answer some days. To have the mindset of Christ means to be kind, loving, patient and gracious with those around you. On your worst days you may find yourself acting in opposition to these traits. We will fail, but today is a new chance to equip yourself with the mindset of Christ. Be in communion with God today through your interactions; let the Holy Spirit flow through you, and allow the grace of Jesus to work through your interactions with others.

READ IT: Psalm 25:1-22

Show me your ways, LORD, teach me your paths (Psalm 25:4).

THINK ABOUT IT: What path are you on? Is it one to which God has led you, or did you take a detour on a path that seemed appealing but distracting? Your heart knows that God's way is always right. Ask God to guide you today. Ask for confirmation that you are going the right way, or ask Him to point you back in the right direction. As your Shepherd, God has promised to never leave you — He is there to guide you today and keep you on the right path.

READ IT: Ephesians 5:8-21

Do not get drunk on wine, which leads to debauchery. Instead, be filled with the Spirit . . . (Ephesians 5:18)

THINK ABOUT IT: Open yourself to be filled with the Spirit today. When the Holy Spirit is in you, you are the person He intends for you to be. Yield your heart and life to the Spirit; place your trust in God, and give Him complete control over all areas of your life. God is waiting for you to choose Him and to allow His power and provision into all areas of your life.

"Your history does not dictate your destiny."

—Sheila Walsh

READ IT: Mark 1:35-45

Jesus replied, "Let us go somewhere else – to the nearby villages – so I can preach there also. That is why I have come" (Mark 1:38).

THINK ABOUT IT: Jesus came so that the world would know the Father and be saved – so that they could know Him forever. That message and that mission did not die when Jesus gave His life for you on the cross. We are also called to go into the nearby villages and preach. Share the Gospel whenever you are able to so that the world may come to know and love Jesus just as you do. Let the joy of the Father be so bright within you that you can't help but share it with those you encounter today!

READ IT: John 14:15-22

" . . . *the Spirit of truth. The world cannot accept him, because it neither sees him nor knows him. But you know him, for he lives with you and will be in you"* (John 14:17).

THINK ABOUT IT: There is a supernatural knowledge and understanding that comes with the indwelling of the Holy Spirit within you. The power, love and righteousness of God so supersedes anything that this world has to offer that many people have a hard time grasping and understanding it. It is only when you live with God fully alive and active in your life that you will know Him in a way that will enable you to share that knowledge with others.

READ IT: Psalm 119:89-120
Your word is a lamp for my feet, a light on my path (Psalm 119:105).

THINK ABOUT IT: What is your source of light in times of darkness? Lean on God's Word today and know that Scripture is a tool for you in all times. It is an ever-shining light to guide you. The light of the Word will shine into every area of your life when you regularly spend time with it. Just like the light of the sun, the light of the Word will help you to grow and flourish.

READ IT: Ephesians 2:1-8

For it is by grace you have been saved, through faith – and this is not from yourselves, it is the gift of God . . . (Ephesians 2:8)

THINK ABOUT IT: The outpouring of God's grace and love over your life is a FREE gift! There is no act that you or anyone else could do to deserve the redemption we are given, yet God blessed us with it by giving us the most precious gift in the world. Receive this gift with open arms and know today that you don't have to try to win God's love, grace or forgiveness, because it has already been given to you.

READ IT: Isaiah 64:1-12
Yet you, LORD, are our Father. We are the clay, you are the potter; we are all the work of your hand (Isaiah 64:8).

THINK ABOUT IT: God is the master Potter, and you are a ball of clay. Open yourself up today and yield your heart to Him so that He may work on you – mold and shape you into exactly what you were meant to be. When you allow God to work in your life intensely, He will transform every piece of you. Trust in His abilities to shape you and your life as you yield your heart and spirit to Him today.

READ IT: Psalm 66:17-20

. . . but God has surely listened and has heard my prayer
(Psalm 66:19).

THINK ABOUT IT: Prayer is so powerful. Your prayers may not be answered how you envision them to be, but don't let yourself be discouraged. Prayer will bring about change. It may be a change in your heart or mind, or in the way you see or feel about a situation. Trust in God's perfect will for your life, and continue praying powerful prayers, trusting that He will always provide.

READ IT: 2 Peter 2:1-22

But there were also false prophets among the people, just as there will be false teachers among you. They will secretly introduce destructive heresies, even denying the sovereign Lord . . . (2 Peter 2:1)

THINK ABOUT IT: If you haven't yet, you will encounter false teachers at some point in your spiritual journey. The only sure way to stand up against their destructive heresies is to have a solid foundation in Scripture. It is so important to have a sound doctrine on which to defend your faith. Continue studying the Bible; regularly read and apply God's Word in your life to strengthen yourself spiritually.

READ IT: Ephesians 3:14-21

. . . and to know this love that surpasses knowledge – that you may be filled to the measure of all the fullness of God (Ephesians 3:19).

THINK ABOUT IT: The love and care of God surpasses human knowledge, but God grants us a spiritual understanding of the depth of His love for us. When you are able to connect with that spiritual understanding, you will experience a fullness and wholeness through God that cannot be compared to anything of this world. Reflect on Paul's prayer today and pray for this spiritual understanding to unlock the fullness of God in your life.

READ IT: 1 John 4:1-8

Whoever does not love does not know God, because God is love (1 John 4:8).

THINK ABOUT IT: It can be easy to think that God doesn't care about you, see you or love you. However, Scripture says right here that God is love. Love is more than what He does; it is who He is. We all fall short of being worthy, yet we have a Father who loves us beyond comprehension. An immeasurable and unfailing love is poured over you today and every day from our gracious God.

READ IT: Psalm 95:1-11

. . . for he is our God and we are the people of his pasture, the flock under his care (Psalm 95:7).

THINK ABOUT IT: The Lord is our Shepherd, guarding and protecting us as His flock. Viewing your relationship with God in this way can open your perspective. Know that He is gentle, kind and caring as your Shepherd. He is there to protect and guide you. As His follower, you should approach Him with love and submission, not arrogance or pride. Trust in His authority over your life today, and believe that He will guide and protect you.

"You can write across
your life: 'Bill paid in
full.' He has paid for
everything so that you
and I can live free of
the shame."

—Sheila Walsh

READ IT: **Matthew 17:1-13**
While he was still speaking, a bright cloud covered them, and a voice from the cloud said, "This is my Son, whom I love; with him I am well pleased. Listen to him!" (Matthew 17:5)

THINK ABOUT IT: How do you handle prayer? Do you feel like you are talking to a distant god who is out of reach, or do you feel like you are in close communication with your Heavenly Father? What a blessing it is to have a personal and intimate relationship with Jesus! Spiritual growth comes through communicating with Him, so challenge yourself to grow spiritually by talking to God as He is: a loving Father who knows you intimately.

READ IT: Hebrews 13:1-5

Keep your lives free from the love of money and be content with what you have, because God has said, "Never will I leave you; never will I forsake you" (Hebrews 13:5).

THINK ABOUT IT: You have everything you need when you have Jesus in your heart. Be content in His presence today, and trust in His promise that He will never leave you nor forsake you. Finding contentment can be a difficult journey, but it is a wonderful place to rest when you lean on His promises.

READ IT: Psalm 34:1-22

The angel of the LORD encamps around those who fear him, and he delivers them (Psalm 34:7).

THINK ABOUT IT: There is nothing you can do and nowhere you can go that will put you out of God's reach or beyond His power, protection or comfort. Just as David cried out to the Lord and was delivered, you can have confidence in God and His love for you today. If you need Him, know that He is there. He is encamped around you, stronger than any forces that may be working against you.

READ IT: Romans 12:9-21
Rejoice with those who rejoice; mourn with those who mourn (Romans 12:15).

THINK ABOUT IT: Christian community is an important aspect of spiritual growth. Who do you share with when you have news to rejoice? What about when you are mourning? Open yourself up to rejoice and mourn with those in your community. Share in the experiences of life and open yourself up to emotional camaraderie. Grow with one another as you rejoice in the blessings of God.

READ IT: Psalm 103:15-22

The LORD has established his throne in heaven, and his kingdom rules over all (Psalm 103:19).

THINK ABOUT IT: Are you trusting that the Lord is in control today? If you aren't living like He is, then who or what is controlling your life? God has an extraordinary purpose to work through your life. Trust in God's control over your life today, and live a life that reflects who is in control. Know that God is working everything for your ultimate good, and believe that it is His Kingdom ruling over all.

MAY
25

READ IT: John 14:23-26
Jesus replied, "Anyone who loves me will obey my teaching. My Father will love them, and we will come to them and make our home with them" (John 14:23).

THINK ABOUT IT: This promise from God simply says that as long as you love the Lord and turn to His Word as your sound doctrine, He will abide in you and with you. Simply by loving God, you will be inclined to obey His teachings and follow His Word for your life. Know today that you are loved by your Father and that He is in your heart. Does your life reflect this promise?

READ IT: **2 Corinthians 4:13-18**

So we fix our eyes not on what is seen, but on what is unseen, since what is seen is temporary, but what is unseen is eternal (2 Corinthians 4:18).

THINK ABOUT IT: Fixing your eyes on the unseen may seem confusing. What this verse instructs us to do, as Paul instructed the Corinthians, is to fix your eyes on the promise of a future with God. The things of this world may seem enticing, but they can't compare to all God has promised you. Fix your eyes on God with faith in Him and the eternal promises He has to offer. The things of this world will fade, but God is eternal.

READ IT: **Philippians 4:14-23**

And my God will meet all your needs according to the riches of his glory in Christ Jesus (Philippians 4:19).

THINK ABOUT IT: What are you needing? Maybe you are lacking the necessary finances to get through the next month. Maybe you are feeling alone and lacking companionship. Whatever needs you feel in your life today, hand them over to God, and trust that He will meet every need. God will always provide for you. You are loved and cared for by a great Protector. Believe that today!

READ IT: Joshua 1:1-9

"Have I not commanded you? Be strong and courageous. Do not be afraid; do not be discouraged, for the LORD your God will be with you wherever you go" (Joshua 1:9).

THINK ABOUT IT: This special promise should be close to your heart. God is so personal that He has promised to be with you wherever you go. When you have the Lord of Lords, Almighty God with you for every step you take, there is nothing to fear. You have nothing to be afraid of, nothing to be discouraged about, because God is on your side. He is with you today. Pray that you will remind yourself of this promise and feel His presence with you.

READ IT: Hebrews 4:1-16

For the word of God is alive and active. Sharper than any double-edged sword, it penetrates even to dividing soul and spirit, joints and marrow; it judges the thoughts and attitudes of the heart (Hebrews 4:12).

THINK ABOUT IT: Where do you turn in times of difficulty? In times of joy? We are told that the Word of God is active and alive. Ultimately, there is no good place to turn in any situation except to God and His Word. It is powerful and able to work in your life and in any situation you may be going through. Challenge yourself to turn to the Word today, and allow its power to work in your life.

READ IT: Philippians 3:12-16
. . . *I press on toward the goal to win the prize for which God has called me heavenward in Christ Jesus* (Philippians 3:14).

THINK ABOUT IT: What race are you running today? Are you working toward your prize in heaven or toward earthly prizes and possessions? Goal setting is a good and healthy habit to have as long as those goals point heavenward, to your ultimate prize. Nothing on this earth, in this life, can compare to what awaits you in heaven. Press forward today with your heavenly goals in mind.

MAY
31

READ IT: Proverbs 15:1-33

A hot-tempered person stirs up conflict, but the one who is patient calms a quarrel (Proverbs 15:18).

THINK ABOUT IT: The Bible tells us that patience is important and useful. When we fix our eyes on Christ and look at the time Jesus spent on earth, we see the depiction of an extremely patient Shepherd. Patience requires self-control and a desire to please God. Pray for patience today. Pray that God will open your heart up to this trait and that you will reap the important benefits of a patient life.